Case Studies for First-Year Experience Students

JOHN RIESEN

JOHN SZARLAN

SUMAN SINGHA
University of Connecticut

THOMSON
— ✦ —™
WADSWORTH

Australia • Canada • Mexico • Singapore • Spain
United Kingdom • United States

THOMSON
WADSWORTH

College Success Manager: Annie Mitchell
Assistant Editor: Kirsten Markson
Technology Project Manager: Barry Connolly
Project Manager, Editorial Production:
Karen Haga
Print/Media Buyer: Karen Hunt

Permissions Editor: Bob Kauser
Production Service and Compositor:
G&S Typesetters, Inc.
Copy Editor: Jan Six
Cover Designer: Lisa Devenish
Cover and Text Printer: Webcom Ltd.

For more information
about our products, contact us at:
Thomson Learning
Academic Resource Center
1-800-423-0563
For permission to use material from this text,
contact us by: **Phone:** 1-800-730-2214
Fax: 1-800-730-2215
Web: http://www.thomsonrights.com

Library of Congress Control Number:
2002108830

ISBN 0-534-26277-5

Wadsworth / Thomson Learning
10 Davis Drive
Belmont, CA 94002-3098
USA

Asia
Thomson Learning
5 Shenton Way #01–01
UIC Building
Singapore 068808

Australia
Nelson Thomson Learning
102 Dodds Street
South Melbourne, Victoria 3205
Australia

Canada
Nelson Thomson Learning
1120 Birchmount Road
Toronto, Ontario M1K 5G4
Canada

Europe / Middle East / Africa
Thomson Learning
High Holborn House
50/51 Bedford Row
London WC1R 4LR
United Kingdom

Latin America
Thomson Learning
Seneca, 53
Colonia Polanco
11560 Mexico D.F.
Mexico

Spain
Paraninfo Thomson Learning
Calle / Magallanes, 25
28015 Madrid, Spain

————————

∞

Dedicated to our former students whose struggles,
dilemmas, and achievements provided the content
for these case studies. And to all future students,
who we hope will struggle less and achieve more
by learning from the experiences of those
who came before them.

Contents

PREFACE

CASE 1   Shock for a First-Year Student   **1**

CASE 2   What Is This Guy Talking About?   **3**

CASE 3   What's the Use?   **5**

CASE 4   Picky, Picky, Picky   **7**

CASE 5   Why Is My Adviser Being So Difficult?   **9**

CASE 6   My Instructor—What a Pain!   **11**

CASE 7   Good Grief! A Teaching Assistant   **13**

CASE 8   What Do You Mean, "Plagiarism"?   **15**

CASE 9   But I've Always Wanted to Be a Veterinarian!   **17**

CASE 10   Nightmare!   **19**

CASE 11   I Have to Write a Paper Too!   **21**

CASE 12   Study Harder   **23**

CASE 13   Academic Trouble—Now What Do I Do?   **25**

CASE 14   Mr. Lucky?   **29**

CASE 15   Confused   **31**

CASE 16   What Have I Done?   **33**

CASE 17   Family Support   **35**

CASE 18   Can I Make It?   **37**

CASE 19 Dead-End Job **39**

CASE 20 Money, Money, Money **41**

CASE 21 He Was My Friend! **43**

CASE 22 She Was My Friend! **47**

CASE 23 Not Again! **49**

CASE 24 My Major? **51**

CASE 25 Math Is Scary! **53**

CASE 26 The Athlete **55**

CASE 27 Chemistry? **57**

CASE 28 Technology **59**

CASE 29 Bad Test Grades **61**

CASE 30 Why Am I Here? **63**

CASE 31 Maybe I Can't Do It Anymore! **65**

CASE 32 What's the Matter? **67**

CASE 33 Roommate Dilemma **69**

CASE 34 I Can't Take It Anymore! **71**

CASE 35 College Is Awesome **73**

CASE 36 Lonely Louie **75**

CASE 37 We Were Just Kidding! **77**

CASE 38 Special People? **79**

CASE 39 He Doesn't Mean It? **81**

CASE 40 Over Coffee **85**

⚸

Preface

TO THE STUDENT

The transition from high school to college is one of the most challenging periods in your life. Moving from a familiar environment where you had a support network of friends and family to a new environment is unsettling at best. Understandably, the challenge faced by each individual varies; however, different groups of students do face some common concerns. For instance, the problems faced by residential students ("I am living with a stranger!") are different from those of commuter students ("How do I ever find a parking space?") or nontraditional students ("How do I balance my family life and school?"). Your situation is also similar to that of other students because you have to perform academically (read effectively, take lecture notes, and prepare for exams), enhance your social skills (deal with the variety of people you will meet and work with), and manage and take responsibility for your own life (balance the many demands placed on you, set priorities, and improve your time management skills).

Although each individual is unique, you and your fellow students will face common challenges in adjusting to college and achieving your goals. In college, you will be faced with the responsibility for and the consequences of the choices you make. You will face challenges of an academic, social, and personal nature, and the choices you make may have long-term consequences.

Although experience can be a very effective teacher, learning by trial and error is not always the best approach. Indeed, too many students are overwhelmed by the many issues that surface and have either left school or done significant damage to their academic record before they have mastered these issues. Case studies provide an excellent means for you to evaluate situations similar to those that many other students face during this period and allow you to evaluate options and arrive at workable solutions. We have prepared these case studies based on the experiences of actual students. Even if you don't experience a particular situation, you can gain valuable insights for your own life from analyzing these cases. Case studies encourage you to become actively involved in your own education.

Often, the challenges that you face will not have simple solutions; they will involve many different players and options. As with most real-world problems, these cases require a systems approach that examines all aspects of the issues, and frequently there is no one right answer. You will have to evaluate the situation, generate solutions, and determine which of these solutions is the most effective and workable. There are few issues in your life that do not involve other individuals, and thus solutions to most problems are not simple. A good way to effectively cope with these situations and issues is to analyze real cases and thereby develop your critical thinking and problem-solving skills. Our hope is that by using this approach you will learn by doing and be better prepared to address the academic, social, and personal challenges that you will face in college. From the discussion of these case studies, we hope you will learn what you need not merely to *survive* but to *thrive* in college.

TO THE INSTRUCTOR

The transition from high school to college is one of the most challenging periods in the life of a student. For the new high school graduate, moving from a familiar environment where he or she has a support network of friends and family to a new and challenging environment is unsettling at best. Although each student is unique, there are common challenges faced by many students in adjusting to college and achieving their goals. Case studies can be an engaging way to take advantage of both the commonality and the uniqueness of students in guiding them to a successful college experience.

Case studies were introduced for classroom use at the Harvard Business School almost a century ago. The case study approach has been gaining popularity with instructors, and the recent focus of higher education on student learning has resulted in greater emphasis on and appreciation for this method. The concept behind this approach is to use classroom discussion to analyze problems and develop potential solutions. Also, the case study approach involves students in active learning. As we move from "teaching" to "learning," it becomes increasingly apparent that case studies are one of the most effective ways to involve students in their own learning. The students move from being passive recipients of information to becoming active participants in the learning process.

Although case studies can be an important tool in most areas of education, they are especially useful in the first year of college. The challenges that students face often do not have simple solutions. They are complex situations involving many different players and options. As with most real-world problems, they require a systems approach that examines all aspects of the issue, and frequently there is no one right answer. Students will have to evaluate the situation, generate solutions, and determine which of these solutions is most effective and workable.

Over the years, all instructors have seen students struggle with many similar problems. Most first-year students will face such challenges starting with their first day on campus. An excellent way for students to cope with these challenges is to analyze real cases and thereby develop their critical thinking and problem-solving skills. Our hope is that by using the case study approach, students will learn by doing and be better prepared to address the academic, social, and personal challenges that they face during their time in college.

This collection of case studies is the culmination of the efforts of three First-Year Experience (FYE) instructors. Each of us has extensive FYE experience and brings a unique perspective and expertise to this project. We believe that although experience is a very effective teacher, learning by trial and error is not always the best approach. Indeed, too many students are overwhelmed by the many issues that surface, especially during the first college year. Using case studies provides instructors with an excellent means for allowing students to evaluate situations similar to those that many of them will face during their college career and allow them to evaluate options and arrive at solutions. Thus, case studies provide a tool for involving students in their own learning and for strengthening their critical thinking and problem-solving skills. We have prepared these case studies based on the experiences of actual students. However, the names and certain other details have been changed to maintain confidentiality. Although many first-year students may not find themselves in the specific circumstances of our case study students, evaluating what advice to provide and learning from the analysis of these case studies will improve their college experience. Furthermore, students are often reluctant to discuss personal problems in a public forum. Case studies provide a situation where they can discuss issues relevant to them, while maintaining their anonymity ("My friend has a problem . . .").

While developing these case studies, we made a decision to select situations that could be presented in a few pages. This allows instructors the flexibility to use them either as homework assignments or in class without prior student preparation.

We know many instructors who are looking to use case studies more extensively but who do not have access to an adequate number of cases. It is our hope that this collection provides a solution to their dilemma. Just as the situations your students will face cannot be neatly categorized, neither can the real-life situations presented in this book. However, in general terms, cases 1 through 13 are academic situations, cases 14 through 32 are personal situations, and cases 33 through 40 involve social situations, skills, and interactions. We hope that both you and your FYE students will benefit from the discussion of these case studies and that they will indeed learn what they need to thrive in college.

John Riesen, Professor of Animal Science
John Szarlan, University Counseling Services
Suman Singha, Associate Dean for Academic Programs

CASE 1

⊗

Shock for a First-Year Student

Sally was in shock! Like all students, she had come to the university with expectations concerning her academic performance and social life. Now it was just the fifth week of the semester, and Sally had received her first chemistry grade. A 55! That was the lowest grade she had ever received. After seeing her grade, Sally's first thoughts were "I don't know if I can do this. Maybe I'm not smart enough. I can't study any harder! Maybe I should just quit. I just don't know what the professor expects from me!"

Sally had been popular and well liked in high school by her teachers and peers and had been active in various clubs and school activities. Academically, she had been a B student.

Her older brother was three years ahead of her and had made the dean's list in two of his six semesters. Although Sally's parents had given her close guidance until she had come to college, she did not feel she could talk easily with them about her grades or what she should do. After all, it was a considerable strain on her family to be paying for two children in college at once. Moreover, they seemed to expect her to follow in her brother's footsteps and do well in college.

Sally estimated her current course grades as follows:

Course	Credits	Estimated Grade
Chemistry	4	F (55)
English	3	C+
Mathematics	3	C−
History	3	D+

ASSIGNMENT

Individually complete the following:

1. State the major problem(s) in this case.

2. List the issues or factors contributing to the problem.

3. What advice would you give Sally to improve the situation?

Work in groups of three to four and discuss the following:

4. What were the problems most commonly identified by group members?

5. What is Sally doing to contribute to the problem?

6. List actions that might improve or resolve the situation.

7. What would be the difficulties with implementing each action?

8. Which action would you recommend be tried first and why?

9. Does anyone in the group know of someone in a similar situation? If so, what has been or is being done to resolve that situation?

What Is This Guy Talking About?

"I give up! I don't have a clue what this guy is talking about!" Peter was frustrated and disgusted. It was halfway through the semester, and he had a 62 on his first exam. The exam had been based principally on lecture material. However, Peter's lecture notes were of limited value.

What made Peter feel even worse was that he went to every class. He tried to concentrate on the lecture and follow what the professor was saying, but he found the lectures fragmented and disorganized. There didn't seem to be a logical progression of facts. Instead, concepts were introduced but never developed. Facts were presented in a seemingly random order, often without relating directly to a concept. At other times, a concept would be introduced, but supporting facts would be presented much later in the lecture without a clear association established to the concept.

"I never had this trouble in high school," was Peter's lament. He would read the text and try to understand the material. The textbook, however, seemed complicated, filled with so many facts that it was difficult to understand. Peter had hoped that the lectures would help him understand the textbook.

ASSIGNMENT

Individually complete the following:

1. State the major problem(s) in this case.

2. List the issues or factors contributing to the problem.

3. What advice would you give Peter to improve the situation?

Work in groups of three to four and discuss the following:

4. What were the problems most commonly identified by group members?

5. What is Peter doing to contribute to the problem?

6. List actions that might improve or resolve the situation.

7. What would be the difficulties with implementing each action?

8. Which action would you recommend be tried first and why?

9. Does anyone in the group know of someone in a similar situation? If so, what has been or is being done to resolve that situation?

CASE 3

☙

What's the Use?

"What is going on?" thought Latisha. "I review the material frequently by asking questions. I know the answers. I take the practice tests in the study guide. I know the answers. My friends quiz me. I know the answers. I teach the material to other students. I take the exam, and I get a D or an F!

"What makes things worse is that when I review the test, I know the right answers, but for some stupid reason, I put down the wrong answer. No wonder I feel anxious when I start to take the exam; I'm trying so hard not to screw up. I usually start okay, but after I miss a question or two, I get confused and begin to doubt my answers. The confusion makes me feel like getting up and running.

"For me, the worst is when I go blank. I feel like I'm staring at a chalkboard that has been erased. I know that somewhere in that chalk dust lies the correct answer, but there is no way my spinning mind can figure it out.

"It's no wonder I'm beginning to feel anxious when studying for an exam that is still two days away. What's the use of knowing the material? I still fail the exam!"

ASSIGNMENT

Individually complete the following:

1. State the major problem(s) in this case.

2. List the issues or factors contributing to the problem.

3. What advice would you give Latisha to improve the situation?

Work in groups of three to four and discuss the following:

4. What were the problems most commonly identified by group members?

5. What is Latisha doing to contribute to the problem?

6. List actions that might improve or resolve the situation.

7. What would be the difficulties with implementing each action?

8. Which action would you recommend be tried first and why?

9. Does anyone in the group know of someone in a similar situation? If so, what has been or is being done to resolve that situation?

CASE 4

⊗

Picky, Picky, Picky

The book closed with a thud. Ahmed had finished another chapter of biology. As usual, he understood little and remembered even less of what he had read. There were so many facts that it was hard to identify the important ones. As usual, Ahmed had highlighted almost everything. There were so many little details. Who would expect him to remember all that material?

About three weeks later, Ahmed found himself two days away from his biology exam. He tried to study the text; each page was a sea of yellow highlighter. With 70 percent or more of each page highlighted, the facts seemed to blend together, resulting in confusion. "Too many details," Ahmed thought, "no one would ask about these picky facts."

A week later, Ahmed looked at his exam grade. "Another F! What is going on? This is the third test I've failed! What am I doing wrong?" Ahmed was confused and frustrated. He was reading all the material, just like he had in high school. In fact, he was studying even more than he had in high school. Yet the exam contained a lot of information he didn't know, and his grades were terrible.

ASSIGNMENT

Individually complete the following:

1. State the major problem(s) in this case.

2. List the issues or factors contributing to the problem.

3. What advice would you give Ahmed to improve the situation?

Work in groups of three to four and discuss the following:
4. What were the problems most commonly identified by group members?

5. What is Ahmed doing to contribute to the problem?

6. List actions that might improve or resolve the situation.

7. What would be the difficulties with implementing each action?

8. Which action would you recommend be tried first and why?

9. Does anyone in the group know of someone in a similar situation? If so, what has been or is being done to resolve that situation?

&

Why Is My Adviser
Being So Difficult?

Nicole was doing relatively well in her classes during the first semester in school, and it was time to select courses and register for the next semester. She thought Dr. Rodriguez was her academic adviser, so she stopped by her office. Dr. Rodriguez was not there, so Nicole left a message on her door. Dr. Rodriguez called Nicole the next day, said that she was not her adviser, and suggested she call the advisory center to determine who her adviser was.

Nicole stopped by the advisory center and was told that her adviser was Dr. Beck. She called Dr. Beck, but he was not in, so she left a message with the department secretary. A few days later, she called Dr. Beck again, but he was not available. Nicole was starting to get frustrated by her inability to get in touch with him. She sent him an e-mail that expressed some of her frustration. Dr. Beck responded that he would be posting the sign-in sheet for advising about registration on his door later that week and that Nicole should sign up for an appointment. The two of them appeared to be starting out on the wrong foot.

Nicole signed up for the first available time slot. On meeting Dr. Beck, she found that contrary to her initial perceptions, he was quite pleasant. Dr. Beck spent time getting to know Nicole and her plans. Following their discussion, he suggested a series of courses for Nicole to take. His recommendations were based on the requirements that she needed to complete for her major. However, Nicole did not want to take two of the four courses he recommended— at least not right away. Dr. Beck felt otherwise, and it became obvious that the two of them were not seeing eye to eye. She argued her case, and Dr. Beck made counterpoints. Nicole felt that her adviser was being unreasonable in not letting her decide what she should enroll in; after all, she was an adult! She was feeling frustrated and decided to end the advising session and think things through. At the end of the session, she was not yet registered for next semester, was finding her adviser to be obstinate, and was frustrated.

ASSIGNMENT

Individually complete the following:

1. State the major problem(s) in this case.

2. List the issues or factors contributing to the problem.

3. What advice would you give Nicole to improve the situation?

Work in groups of three to four and discuss the following:

4. What were the problems most commonly identified by group members?

5. What is Nicole doing to contribute to the problem?

6. List actions that might improve or resolve the situation.

7. What would be the difficulties with implementing each action?

8. Which action would you recommend be tried first and why?

9. Does anyone in the group know of someone in a similar situation? If so, what has been or is being done to resolve that situation?

My Instructor—
What a Pain!

Eric arrived for the first lecture of the introductory course in his major. Dr. Sullivan, the instructor, was already in class and had an outline of the day's lecture written on the board. In the syllabus that Dr. Sullivan distributed, Eric noted that the grading for the course was based on quizzes, exams, and a term paper. There were no points for attending class and, conversely, no deductions for absences.

As Eric, seated in the back row, looked over the syllabus, he thought that this would be a great class. Dr. Sullivan announced that although she had listed office hours in the syllabus, students should feel free to stop by her office any time they had questions relating to the course.

Eric found Dr. Sullivan to be an excellent instructor. Given all the other demands on his time, Eric thought he was doing fine missing only a few lectures and completing most of the reading assignments. However, he never asked questions in class or tried to answer any posed by Dr. Sullivan, and he never went to see her during office hours. Eric was a bit disappointed with the result of the first exam, which was poorer than he would have liked. The mid-term exam was even worse than the first. Eric went to see Dr. Sullivan to argue that she had unnecessarily deducted many points from his mid-term exam. Dr. Sullivan disagreed and told Eric why. Eric thought she was being unnecessarily demanding. Eric's final grade for the course was a C—far below what he had anticipated.

ASSIGNMENT

Individually complete the following:

1. State the major problem(s) in this case.

2. List the issues or factors contributing to the problem.

3. What advice would you give Eric to improve the situation?

Work in groups of three to four and discuss the following:

4. What were the problems most commonly identified by group members?

5. What is Eric doing to contribute to the problem?

6. List actions that might improve or resolve the situation.

7. What would be the difficulties with implementing each action?

8. Which action would you recommend be tried first and why?

9. Does anyone in the group know of someone in a similar situation? If so, what has been or is being done to resolve that situation?

⊠

Good Grief!
A Teaching Assistant

As an incoming first-year student, John was stressed out as it was. Too much was being thrown at him too rapidly. He was trying to adjust to the challenges of having a roommate, eating cafeteria food, and making new friends. He was looking forward to his introductory computer science class. As he sat waiting for the first class, it dawned on him that the large lecture room was filling up rapidly. He had been hoping that the class would be a small one, which would have allowed for more personal interaction. The professor informed them that the course included a laboratory and a recitation section and introduced the three teaching assistants (TAs) who would be in charge of these sections.

John met his TA at the laboratory later that afternoon. The TA was an international student who was working toward a PhD in computer science. He had a definite accent. This was the first time John had been away from home, and he found the TA's accent difficult to follow. John was taken aback when the TA seemed annoyed with the questions he asked. Although the TA was helpful at times, John felt that he was more demanding and less sympathetic than he would have liked. All this was making John feel very frustrated; the linguistic and cultural divide on top of all the other challenges just seemed like too much to handle. John contemplated dropping the course.

ASSIGNMENT

Individually complete the following:

1. State the major problem(s) in this case.

2. List the issues or factors contributing to the problem.

3. What advice would you give John to improve the situation?

Work in groups of three to four and discuss the following:

4. What were the problems most commonly identified by group members?

5. What is John doing to contribute to the problem?

6. List actions that might improve or resolve the situation.

7. What would be the difficulties with implementing each action?

8. Which action would you recommend be tried first and why?

9. Does anyone in the group know of someone in a similar situation? If so, what has been or is being done to resolve that situation?

CASE 8

What Do You Mean, "Plagiarism"?

Erin was a little surprised when Professor Thompson told her that he wanted to see her to discuss the term paper she had handed in the week before. Erin had spent long hours in the library, and she thought it was at least a B paper and was kind of hoping for an A. The tone of the professor's voice, however, and the fact that no other students had been asked to see him made Erin feel quite uneasy when she approached the professor's office later that day. After a business-like greeting, Professor Thompson asked Erin to sit down and made a point of shutting the office door.

"I could have you expelled for your term paper," were his opening words. Erin was caught completely off guard. Professor Thompson then began to talk about options ranging from rewriting the paper to being assigned a failing grade for the paper to being considered for dismissal from school. When Erin finally recovered from her initial shock, she had to ask what the problem with her paper was.

"You plagiarized it!" was the terse answer.

"I cited all my sources; they are all in the reference section," was Erin's response.

"You copied sections directly from the articles," said Professor Thompson.

"How else could I be sure I wasn't changing the meaning of the author?" stated a perplexed Erin.

ASSIGNMENT

Individually complete the following:

1. State the major problem(s) in this case.

2. List the issues or factors contributing to the problem.

3. What advice would you give Erin to improve the situation?

Work in groups of three to four and discuss the following:

4. How would your group define "plagiarism"?

5. What were the problems most commonly identified by group members?

6. What is Erin doing to contribute to the problem?

7. List actions that might improve or resolve the situation.

8. What would be the difficulties with implementing each action?

9. Which action would you recommend be tried first and why?

10. Does anyone in the group know of someone in a similar situation? If so, what has been or is being done to resolve that situation?

C A S E   9

⊗

But I've Always Wanted to Be a Veterinarian!

Jessie had wanted to be a veterinarian since about age 12. She never had a bit of hesitation when asked what she wanted to be; her answer was always, "A veterinarian." She had always had a plethora of pets and seemed to have a way with animals. While in high school, she had volunteered at the veterinary clinic near her home and received compliments from the staff about her performance and encouragement about her goal of becoming a veterinarian. Jessie was well aware that it was a competitive career path, but she knew it was the right one for her.

She took a biology course during her first semester. It was tough and took a great deal of her time. She was disappointed to have a 2.5 GPA at the end of the semester. She was determined to work harder the next semester to improve her GPA. Chemistry seemed to be the main problem during Jessie's second semester. It took most of her time, and although she passed, her other courses suffered as a result. The bottom line was that her cumulative GPA at the end of her first year was 2.6.

The veterinary school at the top of Jessie's list of graduate schools published the profile of its incoming class; the average cumulative GPA for the class was 3.6. Jessie felt dejected. "Should I give up my lifelong dream? Am I not smart enough to get into a veterinary school? What else can I do?"

ASSIGNMENT

Individually complete the following:

1. State the major problem(s) in this case.

2. List the issues or factors contributing to the problem.

3. What advice would you give Jessie to improve the situation?

Work in groups of three to four and discuss the following:

4. What were the problems most commonly identified by group members?

5. What is Jessie doing to contribute to the problem?

6. List actions that might improve or resolve the situation.

7. What would be the difficulties with implementing each action?

8. Which action would you recommend be tried first and why?

9. Does anyone in the group know of someone in a similar situation? If so, what has been or is being done to resolve that situation?

CASE 10

⊠

Nightmare!

Renita was confused. Seven weeks ago, she had thought Professor Nasser's class would be easy. In fact, she had been sure it would be her easiest class. There was no text for the course. All the material would be presented in class lectures. Professor Nasser had all his lectures on PowerPoint™, and the students could download these from the class Web site. From what she had heard, his lectures followed the slides. Yeah, this course would be an easy A.

In high school, she had had a teacher who reminded her of Professor Nasser. Ms. Vega, her high school psychology teacher, would write the main points on the board and provide a few facts to explain each main point. The class had been so easy; each week she would have an exam, which covered the material from that week's lecture. Renita would review a page or two of notes the night before the exam, and she would get an A.

The first few weeks of Professor Nasser's class seemed like high school. His PowerPoint slides would highlight the main points, and Renita would take note of a few additional facts. One difference from her high school class, however, was that Professor Nasser would talk a lot more about each point. He would elaborate on each concept with many facts, which Renita found confusing and not important. Also, he would tell little stories about some of the points, which Renita found entertaining but insignificant. Renita also noticed that after four weeks of class, she had about nine pages of notes and there hadn't been an exam. "This is why college is harder. There is more material covered for each exam. Oh well," Renita thought, "I'll have to study harder."

A week before the first exam, Renita was sitting in class talking with Ian, a third-semester honors student. As the class began, she noticed Ian open his spiral-bound notebook. He opened to approximately the middle of the notebook before he found a blank page. "That's strange," thought Renita, "He can't have 35 pages of notes for this class; I only have around 15. I can't believe he writes down those little facts; no one expects us to know them. He must keep all of his notes in the same notebook. Doesn't he know that he should have a separate notebook for each class?"

The exam was horrible. Fifty questions, all multiple choice; Renita guessed at almost every question. She had studied for two nights and understood the material. Yet on the exam she didn't recognize many of the choices. In fact, she often thought the professor had made up answers. On other questions, Renita recognized concepts but did not know the facts that referred to those concepts. Many of those "unimportant facts" and a few of those "little stories" became answers to exam questions. Answers that Renita didn't know, because she had never recorded the information in her notes. What made matters worse, the final grade was cumulative. Renita's easiest course was becoming a nightmare!

ASSIGNMENT

Individually complete the following:

1. State the major problem(s) in this case.

2. List the issues or factors contributing to the problem.

3. What advice would you give Renita to improve the situation?

Work in groups of three to four and discuss the following:

4. What were the problems most commonly identified by group members?

5. What is Renita doing to contribute to the problem?

6. List actions that might improve or resolve the situation.

7. What would be the difficulties with implementing each action?

8. Which action would you recommend be tried first and why?

9. Does anyone in the group know of someone in a similar situation? If so, what has been or is being done to resolve that situation?

‘

I Have to Write a Paper Too!

The first week of classes had been a big blur for Kevin. He was signed up for 15 credits of course work, and all he could remember of the week was the large quantity of material that had been covered in class and all the reading assignments that he had to complete over the weekend. All this on top of adjusting to college, the time spent commuting, and all the other things going on in his life. He felt that the instructors were expecting too much of him. This was especially true of the instructor in the introductory course in his major, who was basing 20 percent of the course grade on a term paper. Kevin had written a few papers in high school, but the instructions given by Professor Butler were quite specific as to the length of the paper, the format that it had to adhere to, and the due date.

Professor Butler specified that a two-paragraph outline, along with five to seven citations, was to be submitted for her approval prior to the mid-term exam. Only when this outline was approved should the student start to work on the paper. Professor Butler had an open-door policy and told the students not to procrastinate but to start on their papers as soon as possible and to see her if they had any problems or questions.

Time passed very rapidly, and before Kevin realized it, the mid-term exam was only a few days away, and he had not yet started on the outline for his term paper. He knew he wanted to write his paper on biological control of insects, but he didn't know where to start. He felt that going to see Professor Butler at this late date would simply draw attention to the fact that he had not yet done any work. Kevin knew that the Web was a great place to find information, and in less than half an hour he had his outline and five citations.

Kevin was quite unprepared for the comments that Professor Butler made on the outline, which she returned to him a week later. She stated that the outline was unacceptable. According to her, not only had Kevin failed to cite any meaningful references from journals, but two of the Web citations he had used were blatantly incorrect and not based on fact. Kevin was at a loss; he was sure he had read the information on all the Web pages correctly. After class, he looked at the material he had downloaded; which two citations were incorrect? How was he to know? It was on the Web; didn't that mean that the information was correct? He drove home feeling confused and depressed, trying to figure out what he should do.

ASSIGNMENT

Individually complete the following:

1. State the major problem(s) in this case.

2. List the issues or factors contributing to the problem.

3. What advice would you give Kevin to improve the situation?

Work in groups of three to four and discuss the following:

4. What were the problems most commonly identified by group members?

5. What is Kevin doing to contribute to the problem?

6. List actions that might improve or resolve the situation.

7. What would be the difficulties with implementing each action?

8. Which action would you recommend be tried first and why?

9. Does anyone in the group know of someone in a similar situation? If so, what has been or is being done to resolve that situation?

CASE 12

Study Harder

"Not again!" You could hear the blend of anguish and frustration in Rebecca's voice. Rebecca, now in her second year, had been struggling to increase her GPA beyond the C range. Every semester she studied harder and put in more time, yet her grades stayed in the D+ to C+ range. What was especially annoying was that Rebecca understood the material. She could explain concepts to the professor and to other students, yet her grades stayed the same.

If she had studied this hard in high school, she would have been a straight A student instead of having a B+ to A− high school average. It was strange; in high school, if she understood the material, she did fine, but not in college. It was peculiar that the only time her grades improved was on essay exams.

ASSIGNMENT

Individually complete the following:

1. State the major problem(s) in this case.

2. List the issues or factors contributing to the problem.

3. What advice would you give Rebecca to improve the situation?

Work in groups of three to four and discuss the following:

4. What were the problems most commonly identified by group members?

5. What is Rebecca doing to contribute to the problem?

6. List actions that might improve or resolve the situation.

7. What would be the difficulties with implementing each action?

8. Which action would you recommend be tried first and why?

9. Does anyone in the group know of someone in a similar situation? If so, what has been or is being done to resolve that situation?

⚮

Academic Trouble— Now What Do I Do?

Nicholas was depressed. He had come to the university to learn more about dairy cattle management. In high school, he had been popular and had done fairly well academically. However, with his class ranking and SAT scores, he felt fortunate to be accepted to the university. He was proud to be the first member of his family to attend college.

In college, after failing to maintain his GPA at an acceptable level, he was put on academic probation. Then, during the summer before his fifth semester, he received a letter warning him that unless his academic performance improved dramatically, he would be dismissed. Nicholas's reaction to the first probationary semester had been to resolve to work harder, but that had not prevented him from receiving this ominous letter.

Nicholas had had a strong interest in dairy farming throughout high school. In college, he enjoyed courses directly related to his interests, but he had trouble applying himself to the general education courses required for the baccalaureate degree. He worked part time during the semester and full time during the summer on the family farm.

Nicholas' Transcript

FIRST SEMESTER

Course	Credits	Grade
Introduction to Animal Science	3	C+
Basic Writing	3	C
Music Appreciation	3	D
Principles of Biology	4	D+
Semester Grade Point Average	1.123	

SECOND SEMESTER

Course	Credits	Grade
Economics	3	B−
English Composition	3	F
Algebra & Trigonometry	3	C−
Principles of Biology II	4	D
Semester Grade Point Average	1.473	
Overall Grade Point Average	1.323	

THIRD SEMESTER

Course	Credits	Grade
Nutrition & Feeding	3	C−
Independent Study (Milking Management & Mastitis)	2	A
Independent Study (Forage Nutrient Analysis)	1	A
English Composition		AUDIT
History	3	D+
Philosophy and Logic	3	C
Semester Grade Point Average	2.200	
Overall Grade Point Average	1.702	

FOURTH SEMESTER

Course	Credits	Grade
Environmental Conservation	3	D+
Reproductive Physiology	3	INCOMPLETE
Chemical Principles & Applications	4	C
English Composition	3	D−
Semester Grade Point Average	1.400	
Overall Grade Point Average	1.639	

ASSIGNMENT

Individually complete the following:

1. State the major problem(s) in this case.

2. List the issues or factors contributing to the problem.

3. What advice would you give Nicholas to improve the situation?

Work in groups of three to four and discuss the following:

4. What were the problems most commonly identified by group members?

5. What is Nicholas doing to contribute to the problem?

6. List actions that might improve or resolve the situation.

7. What would be the difficulties with implementing each action?

8. Which action would you recommend be tried first and why?

9. Does anyone in the group know of someone in a similar situation? If so, what has been or is being done to resolve that situation?

CASE 14

⊗

Mr. Lucky?

As the anesthetic wore off, Sean could feel the pain in his hand radiate up his wrist and forearm. Through the fog of a hangover, he tried to piece together what had happened at the party.

It had been a good party. The music was fine, people were talking, and everything was awesome. Sean had had a few beers and decided to try the punch. A chemistry major had obtained some alcohol that she claimed was 180 proof. "Funny," Sean had thought as he sipped the punch, "you can't taste the booze."

The rest of the evening was fuzzy. Sean remembered talking with a great-looking girl. Things seemed to be going fine, he remembered, when suddenly he had patted her butt, and she had yelled, "Leave me alone, you pervert." Sean recollected seeing the girl with another guy and getting really pissed off and punching the window. Sean then remembered blood, wrapping his hand in a towel, and riding to the emergency room.

Now, seven hours later, he was sitting in bed trying to consider himself lucky. The doctor said that Sean was lucky; a quarter inch to the left and he would have severed an artery. Instead, he had a broken hand and two severed tendons. The only permanent damage might be trouble grasping things with that hand, but otherwise he would be fine. "I sure am lucky!" thought Sean.

ASSIGNMENT

Individually complete the following:

1. State the major problem(s) in this case.

2. List the issues or factors contributing to the problem.

3. What advice would you give Sean to improve the situation?

Work in groups of three to four and discuss the following:

4. What were the problems most commonly identified by group members?

5. What is Sean doing to contribute to the problem?

6. List actions that might improve or resolve the situation.

7. What would be the difficulties with implementing each action?

8. Which action would you recommend be tried first and why?

9. Does anyone in the group know of someone in a similar situation? If so, what has been or is being done to resolve that situation?

⊗

Confused

April wasn't sure what had happened. It had been a great party. The music was good, the people were nice, and Colby seemed like such a great guy. He wasn't anything like that drunk April had been talking to—the one who punched the window and had to be taken to the hospital. Colby was easy to talk with and was a good listener.

As the evening wore on, April and Colby had become friendlier. They had talked, danced, and laughed. It was after the last drink Colby brought her that April had begun to feel strange. "Strange," she thought, "I only had a few drinks; that last one sure had a strange effect on me.

"I really didn't want to have sex with Colby. I told him no! At least, I think I did? Besides, I was drunk; who would believe me? It would be my word against his.

"I'm so confused, what should I do?"

ASSIGNMENT

Individually complete the following:

1. State the major problem(s) in this case.

2. List the issues or factors contributing to the problem.

3. What advice would you give April and/or Colby to improve the situation?

Work in groups of three to four and discuss the following:

4. What were the problems most commonly identified by group members?

5. What are April and Colby each doing to contribute to the problem?

6. List actions that might improve or resolve the situation.

7. What would be the difficulties with implementing each action?

8. Which action would you recommend be tried first and why?

9. Does anyone in the group know of someone in a similar situation? If so, what has been or is being done to resolve that situation?

CASE 16

⧉

What Have I Done?

April was numb! She struggled to accept the reality of the doctor's words: "Your test results are positive for genital herpes." In a clinical but somewhat reassuring manner, the doctor went on, "There is no cure, but it can be controlled with medication. Of course," the doctor added, "you'll have to be careful."

"Herpes! How did I get herpes?" thought April. "I don't sleep around. There was Jack, my boyfriend in high school, but we broke up last April." And then there was Colby, who she hadn't seen since the party four weeks ago. "Colby," thought April, "I don't even know his last name. And they want to know the names of people I've slept with."

April became enveloped in an empty, sinking feeling. She thought of her parents. They would be so ashamed of her. How could she ever tell them? And what about her friends? Would they think she was stupid, or something worse? Certainly, no man would ever want a close relationship with her. April was disgusted with herself. "What have I done?" she lamented.

ASSIGNMENT

Individually complete the following:

1. State the major problem(s) in this case.

2. List the issues or factors contributing to the problem.

3. What advice would you give April to improve the situation?

Work in groups of three to four and discuss the following:

4. What were the problems most commonly identified by group members?

5. What is April doing to contribute to the problem?

6. List actions that might improve or resolve the situation.

7. What would be the difficulties with implementing each action?

8. Which action would you recommend be tried first and why?

9. Does anyone in the group know of someone in a similar situation? If so, what has been or is being done to resolve that situation?

⊗

Family Support

"I'm not sure I can do this!" You could hear the anxiety and frustration in Debbie's voice. "Two months ago everybody was in favor of me going to college; now everyone is complaining."

It was the seventh week of the semester, and Debbie found herself academically behind and socially isolated. The support of her three children and the significant man in her life had rapidly eroded as the semester progressed. Debbie quickly learned that she couldn't go to classes, read the assignments, do homework, study for exams, write papers, and yet continue to do the same things for the people in her life. Debbie knew college would be demanding, but she had been assured that the individuals who were important in her life would cooperate and help her.

What Debbie found was that her kids still expected dinner complete with homemade dessert, even if there was a paper due. And they still needed rides to swim classes, practices, and friends' houses, even if there was an exam the next week. She found her friends complaining, "You never want to do anything." Then there was the man in her life. Until she began college, they had been talking about marriage; now there was constant complaining about how she spent too much time studying and accusations that she thought she was too good for everyone.

Debbie quickly learned that she couldn't do it all. She tried to be the mom her kids wanted, the friend her friends wanted, and the fiancée her fiancé wanted. On her first exam, she had received her first D. Now she was two weeks behind in course work, physically exhausted, and emotionally spent.

ASSIGNMENT

Individually complete the following:

1. State the major problem(s) in this case.

2. List the issues or factors contributing to the problem.

3. What advice would you give Debbie to improve the situation?

Work in groups of three to four and discuss the following:

4. What were the problems most commonly identified by group members?

5. What is Debbie doing to contribute to the problem?

6. List actions that might improve or resolve the situation.

7. What would be the difficulties with implementing each action?

8. Which action would you recommend be tried first and why?

9. Does anyone in the group know of someone in a similar situation? If so, what has been or is being done to resolve that situation?

⊗

Can I Make It?

Jane could feel her heart pounding as she walked into class. After eleven years, two children, and a divorce, she was finally back in school.

At 18, she had attended college for two semesters. *Attended* was the right word. For two semesters, her emphasis had been social, not academic. Jane had made many friends, joined clubs, participated in college activities, and partied. All those parties! After two socially active semesters, Jane had been academically dismissed—had flunked out! "Looking back on it, at 18 I wasn't ready for college," thought Jane.

Now Jane looked around the classroom with a sense of apprehension and excitement. There was the excitement of taking control of her life, of getting the education that would mean good things for her and the kids. There was also the apprehension and nagging doubts, "Am I smart enough?" wondered Jane. "Can I compete with the 18-year-olds? Can I still be a good mom to my kids? Where will I find the time to do it all? This time, will I make it?"

ASSIGNMENT

Individually complete the following:

1. State the major problem(s) in this case.

2. List the issues or factors contributing to the problem.

3. What advice would you give Jane to improve the situation?

Work in groups of three to four and discuss the following:

4. What were the problems most commonly identified by group members?

5. What is Jane doing to contribute to the problem?

6. List actions that might improve or resolve the situation.

7. What would be the difficulties with implementing each action?

8. Which action would you recommend be tried first and why?

9. Does anyone in the group know of someone in a similar situation? If so, what has been or is being done to resolve that situation?

CASE 19

##

Dead-End Job

Jamaal sprinted up the stairs. A quick glance at his watch revealed he would be 10 minutes late for class again! "The cross-town traffic is always congested and slow," thought Jamaal. The job, however, paid him enough, with overtime, to cover his bills and keep up with tuition payments.

Jamaal had been with the company for eight years and had watched many coworkers with college degrees be promoted while he stagnated in the same job. It wasn't hard to realize that he needed a college degree. With a wife and two kids, his community service activities, and helping his parents, Jamaal's life was crowded with commitments. However, he didn't want to spend 10 years as a part-time student to get a college degree. Ten more years in the same dead-end job would be too much to take. Consequently, Jamaal had decided to enroll as a full-time student and get his degree in four years. It would be a challenge, but he felt that with personal sacrifice and hard work he would do fine. Now, just three weeks into the semester, Jamaal was tired, stressed, and behind in his courses.

ASSIGNMENT

Individually complete the following:

1. State the major problem(s) in this case.

2. List the issues or factors contributing to the problem.

3. What advice would you give Jamaal to improve the situation?

Work in groups of three to four and discuss the following:

4. What were the problems most commonly identified by group members?

5. What is Jamaal doing to contribute to the problem?

6. List actions that might improve or resolve the situation.

7. What would be the difficulties with implementing each action?

8. Which action would you recommend be tried first and why?

9. Does anyone in the group know of someone in a similar situation? If so, what has been or is being done to resolve that situation?

❧

Money, Money, Money

G oing to college was something Heather had always known she wanted to do. She worked hard in school, was active in student organizations, did well on standardized tests, and held a part-time job at the supermarket. She was thrilled when she received a letter informing her that she had been accepted to her school of first choice—the flagship public university in the state. Even more exciting was the fact that she had been awarded an academic scholarship for $1,000 per semester, renewable for the entire duration of her undergraduate studies provided she remain a full-time student and maintain an overall B average. This was a validation of all her hard work.

College started well for Heather, and she immersed herself in academic work and college life in general. She also got a part-time job at a clothing store that was within easy commuting distance of the dormitory. Her incidental expenses were higher than she had projected; the job was ideal and allowed her to earn additional money. Except for her performance in her math course, Heather was pleased with her mid-term grades and with her overall performance.

A few weeks before Thanksgiving, the store manager asked Heather if she would be willing to put in additional hours and help with the Christmas shopping season, especially during the weekends. Heather agreed immediately. The extra money would assist with her expenses and help pay for the presents that she was planning on buying. Two weeks of longer hours resulted in Heather being frazzled, but given that there were only two more weeks of classes until finals, she felt that everything would work out.

It was early January when Heather received her grade report for the semester. She was not pleased with her performance; her grade point average was below 3.0. What hurt even more was that her scholarship would probably not be renewed.

ASSIGNMENT

Individually complete the following:

1. State the major problem(s) in this case.

2. List the issues or factors contributing to the problem.

3. What advice would you give Heather to improve the situation?

Work in groups of three to four and discuss the following:

4. What were the problems most commonly identified by group members?

5. What is Heather doing to contribute to the problem?

6. List actions that might improve or resolve the situation.

7. What would be the difficulties with implementing each action?

8. Which action would you recommend be tried first and why?

9. Does anyone in the group know of someone in a similar situation? If so, what has been or is being done to resolve that situation?

CASE 21

&

He Was My Friend!

"Meredith, is it okay if we tape this conversation?"

Meredith nodded and whispered, "Yes."

"Please start by telling us what happened," said the officer. Meredith sat in silence, trying to make sense of her memories from the night before.

"I've known Stuart for two and a half years. In high school we were on the prom committee together and in the community volunteers club. We hung around with the same people and went to the same events, and our parents knew each other. I remember thinking how glad I was that Stuart was going to the same college. He was a year ahead of me, and I would know someone who could show me the ropes. This doesn't make any sense; I can't believe this happened! I thought he was my friend!"

The woman put her hand on Meredith's shoulder. "I know it's confusing right now. Do you want to take a break?"

"No," said Meredith, "I need to do this. Stuart picked me up around 7 P.M. We were going to the opening performance of the drama club's first play of the year. We have a mutual friend, Ross, who was in the play. We arrived about 7:30 and talked with some people that Stuart knew. It was nice to meet new people; after all, I had only been here a little more than three weeks.

"After the play, Ross invited us to the opening night reception. Stuart knew a few people, and we circulated from one group to another. About two hours later, we left.

"As we headed back to campus, I mentioned how much I had enjoyed the wine at the reception. I had two, maybe three glasses. I remember saying I thought my parents would enjoy that wine. My parents let me have a glass of wine with dinner now and then. Stuart said he had a bottle of that wine in his room, and he would be glad to give it to me for my parents. I thought my parents would like that, and we headed to Stuart's room.

"When we got to Stuart's room, he asked if I wanted to listen to the new CD he had just bought. I asked if his roommate would mind; after all, it was around 1 A.M. Stuart said he was gone for the weekend. So I said, 'Why not, I don't have any plans for tomorrow.' 'Oh, before I forget,' said Stuart and gave me the bottle of wine for my parents and asked what I would like to drink. I was surprised at the amount of liquor Stuart had in his room.

"Stuart made me a drink, and we sat listening to the CD. After a while—15 or 20 minutes, I guess—Stuart leaned over and kissed me. I was surprised, but I found it kind of nice. After all, Stuart was a nice guy and my friend.

"He kissed me again, and this time I kissed him back. From there, it got hotter as we were both into the kissing. Suddenly, he started to unbutton my blouse and kiss my neck. I remember saying, 'Stu, I don't think I want to do this.' He kept kissing my neck and started fondling my breasts. 'No, Stuart!' I said. 'I don't want to do this!'

"'Sure you do,' he said. 'If you didn't want this, you wouldn't be here and you wouldn't have gone this far.'

"At that point, Stuart did what he wanted. I didn't feel I could stop him, so I just let it happen. The next thing I remember was the sun shining through the window and the birds singing. Stuart was sleeping next to me. I put on my clothes and left. I really didn't want to have sex, but maybe I didn't do enough to stop him? I still don't believe it happened. We were friends!"

ASSIGNMENT

Individually complete the following:

1. State the major problem(s) in this case.

2. List the issues or factors contributing to the problem.

3. What advice would you give Meredith and/or Stuart to improve the situation?

Work in groups of three to four and discuss the following:

4. What were the problems most commonly identified by group members?

5. What are Meredith and Stuart each doing to contribute to the problem?

6. List actions that might improve or resolve the situation.

7. What would be the difficulties with implementing each action?

8. Which action would you recommend be tried first and why?

9. Does anyone in the group know of someone in a similar situation? If so, what has been or is being done to resolve that situation?

CASE 22

❧

She Was My Friend!

"Stuart, do you know why we brought you here?" The officer's voice was firm and efficient. "Do you understand the accusations made against you?"

"Yes," replied Stuart, "but I can't believe them. Rape? I didn't rape Meredith!"

"Okay, Stuart, just take it easy, and let's get your side of the events. Is it okay if we tape this?" asked the officer.

"Sure, that's fine," replied Stuart.

"I picked Meredith up around seven. We were going to the opening of the drama club play. We talked to a few people in the lobby before the performance, watched the play, then went to the opening night reception."

"Were you drinking?" asked the officer.

"I had two or three drinks. Meredith had about the same. Neither of us was drunk."

"Okay, then what happened?"

"Meredith and I left the reception and started back toward campus. She mentioned how good the wine was and that her parents would enjoy it. I said I had a bottle in my room that she could have if she wanted. She said yes, and we went to my room.

"I gave her the wine for her parents and we started listening to music. We had another drink or two, and we started to fool around. She was enjoying it as much as I was! We kept fooling around, and one thing led to another, and we ended up having sex."

"Did she say no?" asked the officer.

"She said something about how we shouldn't do this, but when I pushed the issue she just gave in. I thought she was just playing hard to get.

"I mean, she didn't yell and scream, or try to hit me, or kick me where it hurts. She just did it. That isn't rape! I figured some women are passive, and Meredith was one of them.

"Besides, Meredith and I are friends. We have known each other for more than two years. I wouldn't do anything to hurt her. I'm her friend."

ASSIGNMENT

Individually complete the following:

1. State the major problem(s) in this case.

2. List the issues or factors contributing to the problem.

3. What advice would you give Stuart and/or Meredith to improve the situation?

Work in groups of three to four and discuss the following:

4. What were the problems most commonly identified by group members?

5. What are Stuart and Meredith each doing to contribute to the problem?

6. List actions that might improve or resolve the situation.

7. What would be the difficulties with implementing each action?

8. Which action would you recommend be tried first and why?

9. Does anyone in the group know of someone in a similar situation? If so, what has been or is being done to resolve that situation?

CASE 23

⧉

Not Again!

José walked into his darkened room. It was 11:15 A.M., and his roommate was, once again, still asleep. As José closed the door, Christopher stirred. "Hi, José," a sleepy Christopher muttered. "What time is it?"

"It's 11:15," replied José.

"Didn't realize it was that late," said Christopher. "Looks like I missed biology class again. Oh well, it was a nice morning to sleep in. What did I miss this time? Guess I'll need to borrow your notes again."

"No, damn it! Not this time!" exclaimed José. "I am sick of lending you my notes. This is the seventh time in the last three weeks." José was keeping count. "You can get yourself out of bed and get to class or find someone else to use. I get up, go to class, take notes, read the text, I do all the things that a student is supposed to do, while you just lie around, party, and expect me to make up for your irresponsibility! I am sick of it! You're nothing but a f—— parasite! I don't want to be your roommate anymore! I don't want anything to do with you!" José slammed the door as he left.

Christopher was puzzled by José's outburst. After all, José had been lending him his notes since the beginning of the semester without saying anything. José should have said that he didn't want to lend his notes. All Christopher could remember was José saying that he, Christopher, needed to get to class. "José is right," thought Christopher, "but I just have trouble making morning classes."

ASSIGNMENT

Individually complete the following:

1. State the major problem(s) in this case.

2. List the issues or factors contributing to the problem.

3. What advice would you give Christopher and/or José to improve the situation?

Work in groups of three to four and discuss the following:

4. What were the problems most commonly identified by group members?

5. What are Christopher and José each doing to contribute to the problem?

6. List actions that might improve or resolve the situation.

7. What would be the difficulties with implementing each action?

8. Which action would you recommend be tried first and why?

9. Does anyone in the group know of someone in a similar situation? If so, what has been or is being done to resolve that situation?

⌘

My Major?

Christopher went to Jermaine, the RA, to discuss the argument he had had with José that morning. "I don't understand it," began Christopher. "I've been borrowing José's notes all semester and he never made a big deal out of it. All he said was that I needed to get up for class. Then all of a sudden he gets pissed off. I don't understand why he didn't say something sooner. Why didn't he let me know it was bothering him? He could have told me without exploding."

"You're right, Christopher; José could have said something earlier, before he exploded in anger. But you have been missing a lot of classes lately. The first few weeks of the semester you were going to classes; now you just sleep in. What's going on with you?" asked Jermaine.

"I don't know," replied Christopher. "I just don't feel like going to biology or calculus class. I make my psychology and art classes."

"But aren't you a biology major?" asked Jermaine.

"That's what I put on my application. I thought it sounded good, and my parents approved. In high school, I liked my biology teacher. She was really interesting. We would discuss things like global warming and the effects of diseases like AIDS. Now all we do is look at the structure of a cell, or we are expected to learn some chemical cycle. This stuff is boring."

"Have you thought about changing your major?" asked Jermaine. "In a way, it makes sense that you don't want to go to a class that you have little interest in. It sounds like the biology you had in high school is not what they teach here. College is a lot of work! It is important to major in what you want for yourself."

ASSIGNMENT

Individually complete the following:

1. State the major problem(s) in this case.

2. List the issues or factors contributing to the problem.

3. What advice would you give Christopher to improve the situation?

Work in groups of three to four and discuss the following:

4. What were the problems most commonly identified by group members?

5. What is Christopher doing to contribute to the problem?

6. List actions that might improve or resolve the situation.

7. What would be the difficulties with implementing each action?

8. Which action would you recommend be tried first and why?

9. Does anyone in the group know of someone in a similar situation? If so, what has been or is being done to resolve that situation?

⊗

Math Is Scary!

Shawnetta could feel the anxiety rising within her. Her stomach was in knots, and she could feel her heart pounding. This was more than jitters over the first exam. This was the first exam in Math 101.

"Just a review of basic math, some algebra, and a little geometry." That was her adviser's description. For Shawnetta, there was no such thing as basic math. Math was a monster that she feared and tried to avoid at all costs. It was in the sixth grade, more than 20 years ago, that Shawnetta had come to hate and fear math. For more than 20 years, math had intimidated her. Her high school teachers gave her D's in math because she was a good kid, not because she was a good student.

Now, 15 years after leaving high school, in her first semester at college, her adviser described the class as *only* basic math. Shawnetta felt she should be in a remedial math class; however, her adviser insisted that she needed introductory math in her first semester. Taking a remedial class would have put her required math classes out of sequence and postponed her graduation by a semester. "Besides, look at all the other students in introductory math. They may not like math either, but they do it," she'd said. Shawnetta had agreed; after all, she thought her adviser knew what was best.

Now Shawnetta sat staring at the words "Introductory Math Examination" in bold type. Heart pounding, palms sweating, she sat wanting to run, emotionally frozen.

ASSIGNMENT

Individually complete the following:

1. State the major problem(s) in this case.

2. List the issues or factors contributing to the problem.

3. What advice would you give Shawnetta to improve the situation?

Work in groups of three to four and discuss the following:

4. What were the problems most commonly identified by group members?

5. What is Shawnetta doing to contribute to the problem?

6. List actions that might improve or resolve the situation.

7. What would be the difficulties with implementing each action?

8. Which action would you recommend be tried first and why?

9. Does anyone in the group know of someone in a similar situation? If so, what has been or is being done to resolve that situation?

CASE 26

&

The Athlete

The infernal buzzing jarred Sophia awake. In the darkness, she searched for the alarm's off switch. It was 5:30 A.M., an early wake-up time for anyone. For Sophia, a first-semester college student, 5:30 A.M. left her isolated from other students and from the college experience. "The glamour of being a college athlete," thought Sophia.

A 5:30 A.M. wake up gave her time to shower, dress, and grab a quick breakfast before her morning workout. Her body ached from the rigorous training that college athletics demanded. For high school cross-country, she had run 15 miles a week; as a college runner, she did more than 60. Sophia had never felt so physically tired and emotionally drained.

Track practice and meets also took so much time that after five weeks of classes, Sophia knew only a few other first-year students. She felt she was missing the social aspects of college and found herself too tired to enjoy the relatively late night social activities. Besides missing a social life, Sophia felt guilty about her 5:30 A.M. wake up because she often disturbed her roommate.

Sophia was learning that being a college athlete meant focusing on athletics and academics. You knew the other athletes in your sport, and they became most of your social life. Outside of practice you went to classes and tried to keep up with assignments. Mandatory study halls and some tutoring helped, but practice, track meets, and travel made the already difficult college academics much harder than high school. Her A/B average in high school slipped to a C. There didn't seem to be time for everything. In fact, Sophia felt that there was no time for anything.

ASSIGNMENT

Individually complete the following:

1. State the major problem(s) in this case.

2. List the issues or factors contributing to the problem.

3. What advice would you give Sophia to improve the situation?

Work in groups of three to four and discuss the following:

4. What were the problems most commonly identified by group members?

5. What is Sophia doing to contribute to the problem?

6. List actions that might improve or resolve the situation.

7. What would be the difficulties with implementing each action?

8. Which action would you recommend be tried first and why?

9. Does anyone in the group know of someone in a similar situation? If so, what has been or is being done to resolve that situation?

CASE 27

⟡

Chemistry?

"What did I get wrong this time?" You could hear the frustration in Timothy's voice. The results of Timothy's second chemistry exam were back, and Timothy had his second failing grade.

What Timothy couldn't understand was that he kept up with most of the work. He read the text, made up note cards to memorize definitions and formulas, and looked over the sample problems. With the help of other students, he could even solve a few of the problems at the end of each chapter. Moreover, he went to class most of the time and copied what the professor wrote on the board or showed on PowerPoint slides.

Timothy was confused. He put in as much, if not more, work for chemistry than for his psychology and history courses, yet his grades were much worse. He was getting B's in psychology and history. In chemistry, he learned definitions, memorized formulas, and looked at some of the problems. Yet he found that knowing the formulas was of little help, and the test problems were nothing like the ones Timothy had looked at in the text or in his notes. Even more frustrating, Timothy had studied harder for the second test than for the first, and had still received a failing grade!

ASSIGNMENT

Individually complete the following:

1. State the major problem(s) in this case.

2. List the issues or factors contributing to the problem.

3. What advice would you give Timothy to improve the situation?

Work in groups of three to four and discuss the following:
4. What were the problems most commonly identified by group members?

5. What is Timothy doing to contribute to the problem?

6. List actions that might improve or resolve the situation.

7. What would be the difficulties with implementing each action?

8. Which action would you recommend be tried first and why?

9. Does anyone in the group know of someone in a similar situation? If so, what has been or is being done to resolve that situation?

∞

Technology

Greta sat staring at the computer screen. The more she thought about how little she knew, the more anxiety she felt. Just what did the icons mean? Now in her mid-thirties, Greta had been out of school for more than 15 years. She knew returning to school would be difficult, but getting stressed out in the *library!*

At first, going to classes was intimidating, but at least there was a professor who lectured and wrote information on the board. Greta accepted PowerPoint slides as a replacement for the overhead projector and transparencies she had been used to.

Registration for classes had been her first encounter with the computer. At least that time, her adviser did most of the work for her. The adviser not only selected the classes but also entered them into the computer.

Now, sitting in the library trying to research a paper, Greta just had herself and the computer. Modern technology, she was told, had made literature searches fast and easy. You didn't have to review endless index cards in the card catalog, copy your source's title, author, and call numbers, and then search the stacks for the books and articles. With computers, you merely entered your topic, made a few simple commands, and the computer did the work.

Greta continued to stare at the icons. What were those simple commands? And what was her professor talking about when she said she wanted sources that contained scholarly research? What were scholarly sources, and how did you find them?

ASSIGNMENT

Individually complete the following:

1. State the major problem(s) in this case.

2. List the issues or factors contributing to the problem.

3. What advice would you give Greta to improve the situation?

Work in groups of three to four and discuss the following:

4. What were the problems most commonly identified by group members?

5. What is Greta doing to contribute to the problem?

6. List actions that might improve or resolve the situation.

7. What would be the difficulties with implementing each action?

8. Which action would you recommend be tried first and why?

9. Does anyone in the group know of someone in a similar situation? If so, what has been or is being done to resolve that situation?

CASE 29

⽈

Bad Test Grades

Justin was puzzled, frustrated, and although he wouldn't admit it, a little scared. He planned on getting his bachelor's degree and then going to law school like his father, uncle, and older sister. Yet halfway through his first semester, his grades were terrible. Two C's, two D's, and an F wouldn't keep him off academic probation, let alone get him into law school.

Justin couldn't understand the problem. He went to all his classes, read the texts, did the assignments, and studied for the exams. He had even taken a study skills course during the summer to make sure he could study effectively.

Justin wondered what he was doing wrong. "On each exam, I make stupid mistakes," he thought. "I write answers that I know are wrong, confuse information that was easy, and sometimes remember facts after I leave the exam. The only problem I can see is feeling rushed during the exam.

"It's ironic that the exam I failed was the most important one—political science, my major. I really wanted to ace that test! My father and sister received A's in that course. Of course, they received A's in just about everything. Maybe I don't have what it takes; maybe I'm not smart enough."

ASSIGNMENT

Individually complete the following:

1. State the major problem(s) in this case.

2. List the issues or factors contributing to the problem.

3. What advice would you give Justin to improve the situation?

Work in groups of three to four and discuss the following:
4. What were the problems most commonly identified by group members?

5. What is Justin doing to contribute to the problem?

6. List actions that might improve or resolve the situation.

7. What would be the difficulties with implementing each action?

8. Which action would you recommend be tried first and why?

9. Does anyone in the group know of someone in a similar situation? If so, what has been or is being done to resolve that situation?

⊗

Why Am I Here?

"Hey, Mike." Saja tapped on the half-open door. "We have to get to class; our projects are due today."

"I know," mumbled Mike. "You go ahead; I'll catch up." Mike stared intently at the monitor as he tried to break his best score for the computer game.

"Mike?" questioned Saja, "You did finish your project?"

"Not now!" retorted Mike. "I almost have . . ." The screen went blank as Mike missed his chance at bonus points and a new personal best in the game. "Damn, I was so close."

"Mike, what is going on?" asked Saja. "You spend all your time playing computer games and socializing. I bet you didn't finish your class project!"

"Okay, I didn't do the project," said Mike.

"I don't get it," replied Saja. "Going to classes, taking notes, doing assignments—those are your responsibilities. It seems that after the first two or three weeks of the semester you stopped doing anything academic."

"Yeah, I know," replied Mike. "I just don't have any motivation. I plan on doing the work, getting up and going to class, but somehow it just doesn't happen. I find myself doing anything else, making any excuse not to study. I know I am just wasting time and energy."

"Mike, do you really want to be in college?" asked Saja.

"Sure I do," replied Mike, "All my friends went to college. You finish high school and go to college. Isn't that what everybody does?"

ASSIGNMENT

Individually complete the following:

1. State the major problem(s) in this case.

2. List the issues or factors contributing to the problem.

3. What advice would you give Mike to improve the situation?

Work in groups of three to four and discuss the following:

4. What were the problems most commonly identified by group members?

5. What is Mike doing to contribute to the problem?

6. List actions that might improve or resolve the situation.

7. What would be the difficulties with implementing each action?

8. Which action would you recommend be tried first and why?

9. Does anyone in the group know of someone in a similar situation? If so, what has been or is being done to resolve that situation?

CASE 31

❧

Maybe I Can't
Do It Anymore!

Meredith saw the light change to yellow. Almost by reflex she felt her foot press down on the throttle. She knew the light would be red when she went through, but it was 6:15. Practice ended a little after five. Her daughter Beth had been waiting in the cold autumn rain for more than an hour.

As the car sped along, Meredith could feel the anxiety gripping her entire body. After all, it wasn't the best neighborhood. Her thoughts of what could happen to Beth resulted in fear and guilt.

Once again she was late! Late because of her college demands. For weeks, school had been the priority. Everything else had to fit in around school. She hadn't cooked a hot meal in three weeks. Fast food and junk food had become the norm. Meredith couldn't remember the last time she gave the house a real cleaning. Now Beth was waiting in the rain because Meredith had wanted to finish her paper and had lost track of time.

"I sure hope my mother and sister don't find out," thought Meredith. For the past two weeks, Meredith's mother and sister had started to mention that Meredith had been neglecting her duties as a mother. The kids needed more attention and caring. After all, their father saw them only every other weekend. It was their mother's job to raise them properly. Recently, Meredith had also found her mother and sister less willing to help with the kids. "A month ago," thought Meredith, "my mother or sister would have picked Beth up." And her friends Ann, Ami, and Sue could only say, "I don't know how you do it."

"Well," thought Meredith, "maybe I can't do it anymore!"

ASSIGNMENT

Individually complete the following:

1. State the major problem(s) in this case.

2. List the issues or factors contributing to the problem.

3. What advice would you give Meredith to improve the situation?

Work in groups of three to four and discuss the following:

4. What were the problems most commonly identified by group members?

5. What is Meredith doing to contribute to the problem?

6. List actions that might improve or resolve the situation.

7. What would be the difficulties with implementing each action?

8. Which action would you recommend be tried first and why?

9. Does anyone in the group know of someone in a similar situation? If so, what has been or is being done to resolve that situation?

⊗

What's the Matter?

Rachel glanced at her watch as she finished her daily three-mile run. "Still a decent time," she thought, "but I'll need to pick up the pace." As Rachel did her cool-down exercises she could feel the exhaustion moving through her body. "This is how I felt in high school," thought Rachel.

In high school Rachel had run track. Rachel remembered how the coach was constantly pushing everyone to get in better shape and to run faster and faster times. "Her big thing was how much everyone ate and how fat we were," remembered Rachel.

"On her nice days, she would call us big butts, but most of the time it was, 'Hey fat ass!' Regardless of how hard we trained or how much we would diet, she was never satisfied. We were always too slow and too big.

"No wonder at the end of that season, I ended up in the hospital. Exhaustion and malnutrition was the diagnosis. What a senior year! And Mom and Dad wondered why my grades were down. I couldn't run fast enough for Coach, and I wasn't smart enough for my parents."

"Hi, Rachel." The voice interrupted Rachel's thoughts. It was Lindsey and Angela, two of the girls from Rachel's floor. "We're going to dinner; want to come?" asked Angela.

"We'll wait while you shower and change," offered Lindsey.

"No, you go ahead. I'll grab something later. I have a lot of work to do," replied Rachel.

"How can you eat so little and still function?" asked Angela. "Look at you, you're skin and bones; you work out every day, yet I seldom see you eat! What's the matter, Rachel?"

"Nothing is the matter," said Rachel. "I just don't eat a lot."

ASSIGNMENT

Individually complete the following:

1. State the major problem(s) in this case.

2. List the issues or factors contributing to the problem.

3. What advice would you give Rachel to improve the situation?

Work in groups of three to four and discuss the following:

4. What were the problems most commonly identified by group members?

5. What is Rachel doing to contribute to the problem?

6. List actions that might improve or resolve the situation.

7. What would be the difficulties with implementing each action?

8. Which action would you recommend be tried first and why?

9. Does anyone in the group know of someone in a similar situation? If so, what has been or is being done to resolve that situation?

⊗

Roommate Dilemma

Andrew enrolled at the university in the fall and, like all incoming first-year students, was both apprehensive and excited about making the transition to college. Like all new students, he had expectations of how things would be academically and socially. He checked into his dorm room and introduced himself to Austin, his roommate, who had checked in earlier in the day.

Unlike Andrew, Austin appeared to be more garrulous and had already arranged the room to his liking. It also became obvious to Andrew that Austin and he did not appear to have the same tastes in music or level of tidiness. Andrew also discovered in the next few days that whereas he was a morning person, Austin tended to be a night owl and had different study habits. The differences were starting to become stressful to Andrew, and he was worried that he might end up having problems with his roommate.

ASSIGNMENT

Individually complete the following:

1. State the major problem(s) in this case.

2. List the issues or factors contributing to the problem.

3. What advice would you give Andrew to improve the situation?

Work in groups of three to four and discuss the following:

4. What were the problems most commonly identified by group members?

5. What is Andrew doing to contribute to the problem?

6. List actions that might improve or resolve the situation.

7. What would be the difficulties with implementing each action?

8. Which action would you recommend be tried first and why?

9. Does anyone in the group know of someone in a similar situation? If so, what has been or is being done to resolve that situation?

CASE 34

⊗

I Can't Take It Anymore!

"I can't take this anymore!" cried Allison, half shouting, half pleading, as she slammed the receiver.

"Who is it this time, Mom or Dad?" asked Allison's roommate Beth.

"Does it matter?" muttered Allison as she struggled to hold back the tears of anger and hurt.

For two years, Allison's parents had been embroiled in a trying, bitter divorce. Each had assumed an adversarial posture, claiming to be the wronged party seeking justice.

In this emotional quagmire, Allison became the focus of each parent. Both Mom and Dad wanted to enlist Allison's allegiance, while using her as a means to inflict emotional pain on the other. Last in this battle came Allison herself.

In high school, the teachers knew her and her situation. They knew Allison was a good kid who was under a lot of stress, and they went out of their way to help her. Between teachers willing to give her a break and a compassionate guidance staff, Allison had maintained her grades.

College was different, however. The professors didn't know her. Allison found the academic demands stressful and overwhelming. Gone, too, were her friends from high school, and she felt isolated and very alone. As her anxiety increased, Allison found academics impossible. She couldn't focus on lectures or concentrate on her readings. She began to distance herself from other students, at times becoming irritated by the seemingly carefree good moods of others. Why did she have two parents who hated each other and wanted her only for themselves?

ASSIGNMENT

Individually complete the following:

1. State the major problem(s) in this case.

2. List the issues or factors contributing to the problem.

3. What advice would you give Allison to improve the situation?

Work in groups of three to four and discuss the following:

4. What were the problems most commonly identified by group members?

5. What is Allison doing to contribute to the problem?

6. List actions that might improve or resolve the situation.

7. What would be the difficulties with implementing each action?

8. Which action would you recommend be tried first and why?

9. Does anyone in the group know of someone in a similar situation? If so, what has been or is being done to resolve that situation?

CASE 35

College Is Awesome

Morgan walked in the warm September sun, bubbling with excitement and enthusiasm. She had just finished her first week of classes. Finally, she was in college! Morgan wanted to experience it all: classes, dorm life, parties, social and athletic events, clubs and organizations. "It will be like high school, only better," thought Morgan. "After all, there is a lot more time in college to enjoy different activities. Unlike the structured days of high school, with classes from eight to two, in college you're in class only two or three hours a day. Just imagine," thought Morgan, "I have so much more time to do things now than I had in high school. And in high school I got A's and B's, lettered in a sport, was on the yearbook staff and in the outdoors club, and never missed a dance or a car wash."

During the first few weeks of the semester, Morgan immersed herself in college life. She went to classes and did the readings, but unlike in high school, there were no exams, quizzes, or papers due. So far, college didn't seem any harder than high school. Morgan even wondered why she should keep up with the readings, given that she could do all of the work a few days before the exam.

To Morgan, the social side of college was awesome. There were football games, complete with tailgate parties. Social life in the dorms was a stream of conversations; there was always somebody to talk to about any conceivable topic. She could almost feel herself growing intellectually. To keep in shape and to occupy some of her afternoons, she joined two intramural sport teams. And there were so many clubs and organizations that it was hard to decide which ones to join, even after going to the initial organizational meetings. "No wonder college is considered the best years of your life," thought Morgan.

After her first round of exams, Morgan sat in her dorm room wondering what had happened; she had three D's and two F's. "What should I do?" thought

Morgan. "I'm working harder than I did in high school. I went to classes, read the text, and spent a couple of days studying for each exam."

ASSIGNMENT

Individually complete the following:

1. State the major problem(s) in this case.

2. List the issues or factors contributing to the problem.

3. What advice would you give Morgan to improve the situation?

Work in groups of three to four and discuss the following:

4. What were the problems most commonly identified by group members?

5. What is Morgan doing to contribute to the problem?

6. List actions that might improve or resolve the situation.

7. What would be the difficulties with implementing each action?

8. Which action would you recommend be tried first and why?

9. Does anyone in the group know of someone in a similar situation? If so, what has been or is being done to resolve that situation?

CASE 36

⧉

Lonely Louie

Gray clouds sailed past Louie's window. "The clouds are so low, you could almost touch them," thought Louie. He sat, once again, on the window seat looking out over the collection of buildings, trees, and rolling hills that was the university campus. Over the last five weeks, Louie had grown accustomed to sitting and looking. Today the weather matched his often sullen mood. Sheets of cold rain pelted the campus as the university stood shrouded in an autumn gloom.

Like most other entering students, Louie had had expectations of what college would be like. Hard work, yes, but also a lot of fun. Meeting new people, going to parties, games, and social activities, perhaps even meeting that special someone. What Louie found was the discomfort of not fitting in and the loneliness of isolation.

In high school, Louie had had only a few close friends, but in a small town that was enough. He had never been popular and had always had trouble fitting in. Somehow, however, Louie had thought that college would be different. There would be many more people, and somehow he would just fit in. He would naturally make friends and just fall into parties and fun activities. College would just automatically be fun and exciting.

What Louie found didn't match his expectation. His roommate seemed outgoing and friendly at first. After a few days, however, Louie was uncomfortable with the almost constant stream of people in and out of the room. Louie didn't care for his roommate's music, nor his habits, nor the constant chatter. Louie was glad when after two weeks of putting up with this arrogant social butterfly, his roommate moved out.

Louie also became disillusioned with the social life. After two floor meetings and a dorm meeting, he knew three people—two on his floor and one on the floor below his. He went to the meetings and would talk to a few people, but mostly he just stood around. The social activities were similar. He had been to two events, one during the first week, the other an activities night. Once again he had talked to a few people, but no one seemed interested in developing a relationship. Louie had found himself standing around drinking punch and eating the food.

As the weeks passed, Louie spent more and more time alone. Even in his classes he found it difficult to meet people. While other students formed study groups, Louie studied by himself. More and more Louie sat on his window seat and looked out over a campus full of strangers, feeling very alone.

ASSIGNMENT

Individually complete the following:

1. State the major problem(s) in this case.

2. List the issues or factors contributing to the problem.

3. What advice would you give Louie to improve the situation?

Work in groups of three to four and discuss the following:

4. What were the problems most commonly identified by group members?

5. What is Louie doing to contribute to the problem?

6. List actions that might improve or resolve the situation.

7. What would be the difficulties with implementing each action?

8. Which action would you recommend be tried first and why?

9. Does anyone in the group know of someone in a similar situation? If so, what has been or is being done to resolve that situation?

CASE 37

⚸

We Were Just Kidding!

The fall semester started in the usual way, and the first-year students found that many of them were registered for the same classes. This was beneficial because it allowed the students to get to know one another and assist each other in their learning activities in the lectures and the laboratories. As the students started developing friends, it became obvious that individuals who had similar interests associated with each other; and a few of these small groups were all students of the same sex.

Robert had been the 'big man on campus' in high school, having been a good athlete and a leader. Thus, he quickly found himself to be the leader of a group of six freshmen who were impressed with his swagger and attitude. A number of the women in the class were unimpressed with Robert and his group's immature behavior in class and efforts to relive their high school glory days. Although he said nothing, Robert found this lack of adoration disconcerting.

A few weeks into the semester, Robert and his group started indulging in harmless but juvenile pranks, the brunt of which was directed at some of the women in the class. The women largely ignored these. This resulted in Robert and his group starting to interject sexual innuendo when discussing issues with the female students in the laboratories. They were careful not to do this in front of the instructors. Initially, they cloaked these comments as double-edged statements, but they slowly escalated into relatively transparent and disgusting comments. The female students thought that like all juvenile behavior, the crude pranks would soon pass, and they simply ignored them.

A few weeks into the semester, Janet, who appeared to be a major focus of Robert's crude behavior, came to a lecture and went to the seat where she always sat. As she sat down in the chair, it gave way beneath her, and she unceremoniously landed on the ground. This amused Robert and his group, who had positioned the broken chair there intentionally. The class was not scheduled to start for another five minutes, and the instructor was not yet in the room. The hard landing on the floor was a shock for Janet. And coupled with the laughter, it was more than she was willing to accept.

ASSIGNMENT

Individually complete the following:

1. State the major problem(s) in this case.

2. List the issues or factors contributing to the problem.

3. What advice would you give Janet and/or Robert to improve the situation?

Work in groups of three to four and discuss the following:

4. What were the problems most commonly identified by group members?

5. What are Janet and Robert each doing to contribute to the problem?

6. List actions that might improve or resolve the situation.

7. What would be the difficulties with implementing each action?

8. Which action would you recommend be tried first and why?

9. Does anyone in the group know of someone in a similar situation? If so, what has been or is being done to resolve that situation?

CASE 38

⊗

Special People?

Rex was madder then hell! The thought "Enough is enough" kept racing through his mind. This was the third time he had been denied extra help because he didn't qualify for a free tutoring program. The first two times, he had been turned away because the program served a disadvantaged population. This time, the program was for athletes. "Well, enough of this favoritism," thought Rex; he was going to the dean.

Dean Bradley greeted Rex with a handshake and a smile. "How can I help you?" he asked. He could see the anxiety in Rex's face as he shook his hand.

"Dean Bradley, I'm sick of certain people getting special treatment because of who they are or what they do! What about the rest of us?" Rex could feel the anger as he blurted out the words.

"What special treatment?" asked Dean Bradley.

"I've been trying to get tutoring for my Calculus II course, but I'm getting nowhere. My professor is an adjunct and has office hours when I have to work. I work 30 hours a week to pay for college. My parents own a farm and make little money, but I guess that doesn't qualify as a special population," responded Rex.

"What about getting help through the department?" asked the dean.

"They don't have any tutors for Calculus II because of the budgets, *but* they can probably find someone who will tutor me for pay. I can't afford to pay anyone! It's all I can do to pay tuition and expenses. Yet the special people, those who qualify for your programs, get all the help they need," said Rex.

"These programs have specific eligibility requirements that are regulated by federal and state guidelines. If we violated the rules, we would lose the funds and end up hurting students," said Dean Bradley.

"The taxes that my parents and I pay go into those programs, yet I can't use the services. To me, this is a form of discrimination. I guess I don't count because I'm not a member of a special population," Rex responded, and he stormed out of the dean's office.

ASSIGNMENT

Individually complete the following:

1. State the major problem(s) in this case.

2. List the issues or factors contributing to the problem.

3. Is Rex prejudiced? What is the basis for your answer?

Work in groups of three to four and discuss the following:

4. What were the problems most commonly identified by group members?

5. Is the above situation fair? Should certain groups be provided special programs and services?

6. How can the situation be improved?

7. If you were Dean Bradley, what would you do?

8. Why are accommodations and services provided to certain individuals?

⊗

He Doesn't Mean It?

The three couples were looking forward to the concert. Not only were they going to see their favorite group, but they had seats in the third row. Kelly knew the wife of a musician from a rock group used to introduce the featured group.

Kelly was a first-year student and had been going out with Dylan for two and a half months. Dylan was in his third semester and was friends with Raoul and Jody, both in their fifth semester. The other couple was Sasha and Derek. Sasha lived down the hall from Kelly, and Derek knew Jody. None of the couples had ever gone out together.

The couples made their way to the seats just before the intro group began to play. Rico, the musician who had gotten Kelly the tickets, noticed her and came over.

"Glad to see you made it," said Rico.

"We wouldn't miss this," said Kelly. "Thank you so much. I don't know how to repay you."

After a quick round of introductions, Rico gave Kelly a hug and went back on stage. The couples settled in and for three hours listened to the music and watched the show.

After the concert, the couples decided to stop and have pizza. They made their way to a large booth in the corner. The group chatted about the concert and what a great performance it had been. Derek mentioned that Rico seemed like a nice guy and asked Kelly how long she had known him.

As Kelly started to respond, Dylan interrupted, "You seem to like that guy, Rico?" His tone indicated more than a casual question.

"Rico is a nice guy, but I know him through his wife, Judy. Judy and I have been friends for five years or so." Kelly seemed a little defensive.

"Well, the way you hugged Rico, I thought you two had something going!" Dylan stared at Kelly.

"Dylan, don't start! Rico and I . . ." Her words ended abruptly as Dylan grabbed the back of Kelly's head and pulled her toward him.

"You don't tell me anything!" Dylan's words cut like a knife as he glared at Kelly. "No female tells me anything! You got that, bitch?"

"Dylan, you're hurting me! Please stop!" Kelly's voice was a fearful mix of request and pleading. She tried to push Dylan's hand away.

The other couples sat stunned, each trying to decide how best to stop this situation before it got worse.

"Hey, Dylan, I'm sure she didn't mean anything by it," Raoul tried to break the sudden tension. "Come on, give me a hand to get the pizza and drinks."

"Yeah, let's go get the food, Dylan, okay?" asked Derek.

Slowly, Dylan released Kelly. "Okay, let's get the food," he said.

As the guys left the table, Kelly tried to compose herself and hide her embarrassment and anxiety.

"Are you okay?" asked Jody.

Kelly gave a quick nod as she tried to fix her hair.

"Has he ever done that before?" probed Sasha.

"He doesn't mean anything by it," replied Kelly. "You watch; he will be real nice the rest of the evening. He just gets angry sometimes and has trouble controlling it. A lot of the time, he doesn't even remember everything that happened. It's just that he cares so much for me that he has trouble controlling his emotions."

"Bullshit," responded Sasha. "No one has the right to abuse another person. What I saw was verbal abuse, along with physical abuse. Has he ever hit you?"

Kelly's gaze shifted to the floor. "No," was her muffled response.

"I don't believe you!" Sasha shot back. "Does this guy make you do things you don't want to do?"

Kelly's eyes stayed fixed on the floor.

"Kelly, this is abuse," pleaded Jody. "You don't have to take this! No one has the right to treat another person this way!"

By this time, Dylan had been escorted to a quiet corner by Raoul and Derek.

"What was that about, Dylan?" Raoul and Derek both looked puzzled and upset.

"What was what? Kelly is my woman; I just need to keep her in line," retorted Dylan.

"That's abuse, Dylan! You can't do that to people," said Raoul.

"Hey!" Dylan pointed his finger at Raoul's face, "I will do what I want; she is my woman! And you keep your nose out of my business, or I'll straighten you out too."

"Dylan," Derek stepped between them, not wanting the situation to escalate. "Dylan, calm down. Your anger isn't going to help you or anyone. Please calm down."

Slowly, Dylan lowered his finger.

"Hey, I have a short fuse! So what?" His question was really a statement. "That's just the way I am, and people have to take me how I am, right? Right!"

"Dylan, you have a problem with anger. You lose control too easily and too often. That may be the way you are, but that doesn't mean others have to tolerate you," responded Raoul.

"Hey, I'm not that bad," responded Dylan. "Besides, I come from a culture where men are supposed to be aggressive; it's our pride. I don't take anybody's crap! That's the way I was raised."

ASSIGNMENT

Individually complete the following:

1. State the major problem(s) in this case.

2. List the issues or factors contributing to the problem.

3. What advice would you give Kelly and/or Dylan to improve the situation?

Work in groups of three to four and discuss the following:

4. What were the problems most commonly identified by group members?

5. What are Kelly and Dylan each doing to contribute to the problem?

6. List actions that might improve or resolve the situation.

7. What would be the difficulties with implementing each action?

8. Which action would you recommend be tried first and why?

9. Does anyone in the group know of someone in a similar situation? If so, what has been or is being done to resolve that situation?

CASE 40

⊗

Over Coffee

Kasha burst through the tutoring office door. "I'm sorry! I know I'm late for work again," apologized Kasha, who had started working as a peer tutor a month ago.

"Slow down," said Jennifer. "It's only 10 after. Come on, let's sit down and have a cup of coffee. With the bad weather, no one is coming for tutoring. Besides, you're soaked from being in the rain."

"When you walk half a mile from the parking lot, you're going to get wet!" exclaimed Kasha. "And that parking lot gets further away every time I'm running late."

"I know; it takes forever to get to class, especially when you're carrying a lot of books," empathized Jennifer. "Let's just sit and relax for a few minutes. Here's your coffee."

"Thanks," said Kasha. "Have you heard from State yet?"

"Not yet, but I'm keeping my fingers crossed," said Jennifer. "It's the only school within driving distance that has the program I want. My husband and kids are not about to move so I can go to school. The last two years have been great, but in my field, a two-year degree doesn't mean much."

"I'm sure you'll get in. A 3.7 GPA is hard to ignore," said Kasha.

"I think I have a good chance, but I'm not sure how many of my credits will transfer. I may have messed up my first semester or two by not checking the courses I was taking. Some of them may not have had the right content. I should have questioned my adviser more about whether the courses would transfer. It was my responsibility to check, and I didn't. At my age, I don't want to spend any more time in school than I have to," said Jennifer. "What about you, Kasha? How is your first year going?"

"You mean besides feeling overwhelmed, overworked, and without enough time for myself? I guess like everybody else, I'm having trouble finding time to do it all. Since my son went into counseling, it has been better. Before counseling, I never knew what to expect when I got home. Thank goodness I went to the college's substance abuse center for a referral. Of course, that's why I'm running late today; his session ran late. Between the individual sessions and the group meetings, I have more driving to do," said Kasha.

"Can't anyone help you with some of the outside things?" asked Jennifer.

"Nah, his father is always too busy or has something to do. I don't like asking my family and friends, because they have lives of their own. No, I'll just make do," replied Kasha.

"Have you checked with community services or counseling? They are familiar with various community resources that may be able to help you. Who knows, maybe if you talked with someone, things wouldn't seem so overwhelming? Why don't you give it a try?" suggested Jennifer.

"I never gave that a thought. Maybe they can help with the situation. Thanks for the idea, Jennifer."

ASSIGNMENT

Individually complete the following:

1. State the major problem(s) in this case.

2. List the issues or factors contributing to the problem.

3. What advice would you give Kasha to improve the situation?

Work in groups of three to four and discuss the following:

4. What were the problems most commonly identified by group members?

5. What is Kasha doing to contribute to the problem?

6. List actions that might improve or resolve the situation.

7. What would be the difficulties with implementing each action?

8. Which action would you recommend be tried first and why?

9. Does anyone in the group know of someone in a similar situation? If so, what has been or is being done to resolve that situation?

10. Do you agree that Jennifer is at fault for having taken the wrong courses? How can a student learn about transfer policies of a particular school and what courses might transfer?

Topical Index of Cases

Following each topic are cases that could be used to introduce or amplify that topic.

Abusive relationships, Case 39
Academic adviser, Case 5
Academic skills, Cases 13 and 29
Adjustment period, Case 36
Alcohol induced behavior,
    Cases 14 and 15
Anger management, Case 39
Assertiveness, Case 23
Athletes, Case 26
Attendance, Case 6
Attitude, Case 37

Balancing commitments,
    Cases 17, 18, 19, 20, 26, 28,
    31, 35, and 40

Campus policies, Cases 8 and 13
Campus resources, Cases 15,
    16, 21, 24, and 40
Career choices, Cases 9 and 24
Career decisions/goals, Case 13
Co-curricular activities,
    Case 35
Communication skills, Cases 7,
    23, 33, and 37
Computer technology/skills,
    Case 28
Conflict resolution, Cases 23,
    24, 34, and 38
Consequences of drinking,
    Cases 14 and 15
Course selection, Case 5
Cultural differences, Cases 7
    and 39

Date rape, Cases 14, 15, 21,
    and 22
Dealing with diverse individu-
    als, Cases 7, 38, and 39
Decision making, Case 24
Declaring a major, Case 24
Demands of college, Cases 20
    and 24
Depression, Cases 32 and 36
Diversity, Case 7

Eating disorders, Case 32
Effective communication,
    Case 22
Emotional problems, Cases 32,
    34, and 37

Essay exams, Case 12
Exam expectations vs. reality,
    Cases 6, 10, and 25
Expectations, Cases 1, 6, 9, 17,
    29, 30, 31, and 34

Family obligations/expecta-
    tions, Cases 1, 17, 29, 31,
    and 34
Freedom in college, Cases 5
    and 35

GPA (grade point average),
    Cases 9 and 13
Graduation requirements,
    Cases 5 and 9

Harassment, Cases 37 and 39
Health issues, Cases 16 and 32
High school vs. college, Cases
    1, 3, 4, 10, 11, and 12

Interpersonal skills, Cases 21,
    22, 23, 31, 33, 34, 36, 37,
    and 39

Juggling school and family,
    Cases 17, 31, and 40

Learning disabled students,
    Case 38
Learning styles, Cases 2, 4, 10,
    12, 27, and 29
Lecture notes, Cases 2, 10, and
    27
Living styles, Case 33

Math anxiety, Case 25
Money management, Cases 1
    and 20
Motivation/goals, Cases 26
    and 30
Multiple-choice exams, Case 12

Nontraditional students, Cases
    17, 18, 19, 25, 28, 31, and 40
Note-taking skills, Case 27

Office hours, Case 6
Outlines, Case 11
Outlining, Case 4

Personal responsibility,
    Case 38
Plagiarism, Case 8
Procrastination, Case 11

Reasons for going to college,
    Cases 1 and 30
Reference citation, Cases 8, 11,
    and 28
Relationships, Cases 17, 21, 22,
    and 39
Residence life, Cases 33 and 36
Returning-student issues,
    Cases 18 and 28
Review strategies, Cases 4 and
    10
Roommate issues, Cases 23, 24,
    and 33

Safe sex, Case 16
Sexism, Cases 37 and 39
Sexual aggression/harassment,
    Case 37
Sexual assault, Cases 17, 21,
    and 22
Social skills, Cases 14 and 36
STDs, Case 16
Stress management, Cases 7,
    19, 26, 33, 34, and 40
Structuring and organizing in-
    formation, Cases 2 and 4
Student-faculty relationship,
    Case 6
Study skills, Cases 2, 12, and 27
Substance abuse, Case 14

Test anxiety, Cases 3, 25, 27,
    and 29
Test-taking skills, Cases 3, 4,
    27, and 29
Text notes, Cases 4 and 27
Time management, Cases 20,
    26, 35, and 40

Web resources, Cases 11 and
    28
Web technology, Case 28
Working students, Cases 19,
    20, and 38
Writing a term paper, Cases 8
    and 11